LEGACY BUILDERS

Creating Wealth for Future Generations

CHRIS JOSH

Copyright © 2024 by Chris Josh

TABLE OF CONTENT

INTRODUCTION 5

CHAPTER 1: DEFINING YOUR LEGACY 8

- The Concept of Legacy 10

- Reflecting on Your Values and Beliefs 13

- Setting Clear Objectives for Your Legacy
Building Journey 17

CHAPTER 2: CULTIVATING A PROSPERITY
MINDSET 23

- The Psychology of Wealth 25

- Overcoming Limiting Beliefs and Mindset
Blocks 29

- Adopting Habits and Practices That Foster
Financial Abundance 34

CHAPTER 3: ETHICAL STEWARDSHIP AND
RESPONSIBLE WEALTH MANAGEMENT 40

- The Intersection of Ethics and Wealth 43

Implementing Sustainable Investment Strategies
.... 47

- Navigating the Complexities of Wealth Transfer and Inheritance 53

CHAPTER 4: INTEGRATING PHILANTHROPY INTO YOUR LEGACY 59

- The Power of Giving Back 61

- Identifying Causes and Organizations That Align with Your Values 66

- Leveraging Philanthropy as a Catalyst for Social Impact 70

CHAPTER 5: NURTURING INTERGENERATIONAL COLLABORATION. 76

- Fostering Open Dialogue Within Your Family 79

- Passing Down Values, Wisdom, and Lessons Learned 84

- Collaborating Across Generations to Sustain and Enhance Your Legacy 89

CONCLUSION 95

INTRODUCTION

In the timeless pursuit of leaving a lasting impact, the concept of legacy resonates deeply within us. Legacy transcends mere material possessions; it embodies values, principles, and the imprints of our actions that endure beyond our lifetime. "Legacy Builders: Creating Wealth for Future Generations" serves as a guiding beacon for individuals aspiring to craft a legacy of significance, one that transcends generations and leaves an indelible mark on the world.

In this book, we embark on a transformative journey that transcends conventional notions of wealth. While financial prosperity is undeniably a crucial aspect, true legacy building encompasses a holistic approach that encompasses emotional, intellectual, and spiritual wealth. We delve into the depths of what it means to build a legacy that enriches the lives of not just our descendants but also the broader community and society at large.

Drawing from the wisdom of history's most renowned legacy builders and modern-day visionaries, "Legacy Builders" presents a comprehensive framework for creating sustainable wealth that endures over time. Through insightful anecdotes, practical strategies, and thought-provoking exercises, readers are empowered to define their unique legacy and chart a course towards its realization.

Key themes explored within these pages include the cultivation of a prosperity mindset, the importance of ethical stewardship, and the integration of philanthropy into wealth management practices. Furthermore, we address the vital role of intergenerational communication and collaboration in preserving and enhancing the legacy for future generations.

Whether you are a seasoned entrepreneur, a seasoned investor, a philanthropist, or simply an individual seeking to make a meaningful difference, "Legacy Builders" provides invaluable insights and actionable guidance to ignite your journey towards creating a legacy that transcends time. Together, let us embark on this profound odyssey of legacy building, where each decision we make today echoes into eternity, shaping a brighter tomorrow for generations yet to come.

CHAPTER 1: DEFINING YOUR LEGACY

Embarking on the journey of legacy building begins with a fundamental step: defining what legacy means to you. In this pivotal chapter, we delve into the intricate process of self-reflection and introspection to uncover the essence of your legacy. Forging a clear understanding of your aspirations, values, and intentions lays the groundwork for crafting a legacy that resonates with your true essence and leaves a profound impact on future generations.

Within these pages, we invite you to embark on a deeply personal exploration, guided by thought-provoking questions and reflective exercises. By engaging in this introspective journey, you will gain clarity on what matters most to you and how you envision your legacy unfolding. Whether your aspirations revolve around leaving a financial inheritance, making a difference in your community, or imparting timeless wisdom to your descendants, this chapter provides a roadmap for translating your aspirations into actionable objectives.

Moreover, we recognize that the concept of legacy is fluid and evolves. As such, we encourage you to embrace the process of continual refinement and adaptation, allowing your legacy to grow and evolve alongside your growth journey. By defining your legacy with intentionality and authenticity, you pave the way for a purpose-driven life that extends far beyond your existence.

As we embark on this transformative journey of self-discovery and vision-setting, remember that your legacy is a testament to the values you hold dear and the impact you aspire to make. Through introspection and intentionality, you possess the power to shape a legacy that embodies your essence and leaves an enduring mark on the world. Let us embark on this profound odyssey of self-discovery and legacy crafting, where each moment of reflection brings us closer to realizing our deepest aspirations.

- The Concept of Legacy

The concept of legacy is multifaceted, encompassing various dimensions of human existence, including but not limited to, material wealth, intellectual contributions, values, and cultural heritage. At its core, legacy refers to the imprint that individuals leave behind as a result of their actions, beliefs, and achievements. It transcends the boundaries of time, extending far beyond an individual's lifetime to shape the course of future generations and influence the broader tapestry of society. To comprehensively discuss the concept of legacy, it's essential to explore its key components and significance:

1. **Material Legacy**: This aspect of legacy typically pertains to tangible assets, such as wealth, property, and possessions, passed down from one generation to the next. While material inheritance is often a significant component of legacy, it is not the sole

determinant of an individual's impact. The responsible stewardship of material wealth and its alignment with the values and aspirations of the benefactor are equally crucial.

2. **Intellectual Legacy:** Intellectual contributions encompass the knowledge, ideas, and innovations that individuals contribute to their fields of expertise or humanity as a whole. This can include scientific discoveries, artistic creations, literary works, and philosophical insights. Intellectual legacies endure through their influence on future generations, shaping thought, inspiring creativity, and advancing human progress.

3. **Values and Principles:** Beyond material and intellectual wealth, legacy is deeply intertwined with the values, principles, and beliefs that individuals embody and pass down to subsequent generations. These values serve as guiding lights, shaping the moral compass of individuals and communities, and informing decision-making processes. The transmission of core values from one

generation to the next is essential for preserving cultural identity and fostering social cohesion.

4. **Cultural Legacy**: Cultural heritage encompasses traditions, rituals, languages, arts, and customs that define the identity of a community or civilization. Individuals contribute to cultural legacy through their participation in and preservation of cultural practices, as well as through the creation of cultural artefacts that endure over time. Cultural legacies serve as bridges between the past, present, and future, connecting individuals to their roots while facilitating cultural exchange and understanding.

5. **Humanitarian and Philanthropic Legacy:** Another dimension of legacy involves the impact individuals make through acts of kindness, service, and philanthropy. Whether through charitable giving, community service, or advocacy for social justice, individuals can leave a lasting legacy of compassion and altruism that improves the lives of others and contributes to the betterment of society.

In summary, the concept of legacy encompasses a rich tapestry of material, intellectual, moral, cultural, and humanitarian contributions that individuals leave behind as their enduring mark on the world. It reflects not only what individuals achieve during their lifetimes but also how they choose to live, the values they uphold, and the impact they make on future generations. By consciously cultivating a legacy aligned with their deepest values and aspirations, individuals have the power to shape a brighter, more meaningful future for themselves and those who follow in their footsteps.

- Reflecting on Your Values and Beliefs

Reflecting on your values and beliefs is a deeply introspective process that involves examining the core principles, convictions, and ethical standards that guide your thoughts, actions, and decisions. This introspection is essential for gaining clarity on what truly matters to you, understanding your motivations, and aligning your behaviors with your authentic self. A comprehensive discussion of reflecting on your values and beliefs involves exploring their importance, methods, and potential outcomes:

1. Importance of Reflection:

- **Clarifying Personal Identity**: Reflecting on values and beliefs helps individuals understand who they are at their core, enabling them to define their identity and sense of self.

- **Guiding Decision Making:** Your values and beliefs serve as a compass, providing guidance and direction when faced with life's choices and challenges.

- **Enhancing Well-being**: Living in alignment with your values fosters a sense of authenticity, fulfilment, and inner peace, promoting overall psychological well-being.

2. **Methods of Reflection:**

- **Journaling:** Writing down your thoughts, feelings, and reflections in a journal allows for deeper introspection and self-exploration.

- **Mindfulness Practices**: Engaging in mindfulness meditation or other contemplative practices can help quiet the mind and facilitate introspective insights.

- **Seeking Feedback**: Soliciting feedback from trusted friends, family members, or mentors can provide valuable perspectives on your values and beliefs.

3. **Exploring Values and Beliefs**:

- **Core Values**: Identify the principles and ideals that are most important to you, such as honesty, integrity, compassion, or personal growth.

- **Origin and Influence**: Reflect on the origins of your values and beliefs, considering how they were shaped by your upbringing, culture, experiences, and influential figures in your life.

- **Consistency and Alignment**: Assess whether your behaviors and decisions align with your professed values and beliefs, identifying areas where there may be discrepancies or conflicts.

4. Challenging Assumptions and Evolving Perspectives:

- **Questioning Assumptions**: Challenge ingrained beliefs and assumptions, remaining open to new perspectives and experiences that may broaden your understanding and worldview.

- **Embracing Growth**: Recognize that values and beliefs are not static; they can evolve as you gain new insights, experiences, and knowledge.

5. Potential Outcomes:

- **Greater Clarity and Purpose**: Reflecting on your values and beliefs can provide clarity on your life's purpose and priorities, empowering you to live authentically and with intention.

- **Enhanced Relationships**: Understanding your values and beliefs can foster deeper connections and more meaningful relationships with others who share similar convictions.

 - **Improved Decision Making**: Making decisions that align with your values leads to greater satisfaction and a sense of fulfillment, as you honor your authentic self.

In conclusion, reflecting on your values and beliefs is a transformative process that enables self-discovery, personal growth, and alignment with your true essence. By engaging in this introspective journey, you can cultivate a more authentic and purposeful life that resonates with your deepest convictions and aspirations.

- Setting Clear Objectives for Your Legacy Building Journey

Setting clear objectives for your legacy-building journey is a crucial step in ensuring that your efforts are focused, purposeful, and aligned with your values and aspirations. This comprehensive discussion will explore the importance of setting objectives, strategies for defining them, and the potential impact they can have on your legacy:

1. **Importance of Setting Objectives**:

 - **Direction and Focus**: Clear objectives provide a roadmap for your legacy-building journey, guiding your actions and decisions toward a specific outcome.

 - **Motivation and Accountability**: Having well-defined objectives can serve as a source of motivation, inspiring you to take consistent action toward achieving your desired legacy. Additionally, clear objectives create accountability, as you can track your progress and make adjustments as needed.

 - **Alignment with Values**: Objectives should reflect your core values and beliefs, ensuring that your legacy-building efforts are authentic and meaningful.

2. Strategies for Defining Objectives:

- Reflect on Your Values and Aspirations: Begin by reflecting on what matters most to you and what you hope to achieve through your legacy. Consider the impact you want to make on future generations and the values you want to instil.

- Set Specific, Measurable, Achievable, Relevant, and Time-bound (SMART) Goals: Define objectives that are specific, measurable, achievable, relevant, and time-bound. For example, instead of a vague goal like "leaving a positive impact," set a specific goal such as "establishing a scholarship fund to support underprivileged students within the next five years."

- Prioritize Objectives: Identify the most important objectives that will have the greatest impact on your legacy. Prioritizing objectives can help you focus your time and resources on activities that align with your overarching goals.

3. **Types of Objectives:**

  - **Financial Objectives**: These objectives may include accumulating a certain amount of wealth to pass on to future generations, establishing a family foundation, or creating a trust fund for charitable purposes.

  - **Philanthropic Objectives**: Philanthropic objectives involve giving back to society through charitable donations, volunteering, or supporting causes that align with your values and beliefs.

  - **Educational Objectives**: Educational objectives focus on fostering learning and personal development, such as providing scholarships, funding educational programs, or supporting research initiatives.

  - **Cultural or Environmental Objectives**: These objectives aim to preserve and promote cultural heritage, protect the environment, or contribute to the arts and humanities.

4. Evaluating and Adjusting Objectives:

- Regularly evaluate your progress toward achieving your objectives, assessing whether you are on track to meet your goals.

- Be open to adjusting your objectives as circumstances change or new opportunities arise. Flexibility is key to adapting your legacy-building strategy to evolving needs and priorities.

5. Potential Impact of Objectives on Your Legacy:

- **Creating a Lasting Impact:** Clear objectives increase the likelihood of creating a legacy that endures beyond your lifetime, positively impacting future generations.

- **Inspiring Others:** By setting ambitious objectives and taking intentional action to achieve them, you can inspire others to follow in your footsteps and contribute to meaningful change.

- **Building a Meaningful Legacy:** Objectives that are aligned with your values and aspirations contribute to building a legacy that reflects your authentic self and leaves a lasting imprint on the world.

In summary, setting clear objectives for your legacy-building journey is essential for providing direction, focus, and accountability. By defining objectives that align with your values and aspirations, you can create a meaningful legacy that positively impacts future generations and reflects the essence of who you are.

CHAPTER 2: CULTIVATING A PROSPERITY MINDSET

In the pursuit of building a lasting legacy, the mindset we cultivate plays a pivotal role in shaping our journey towards success and fulfillment. The concept of a prosperity mindset transcends mere financial wealth; it encompasses a mindset of abundance, resilience, and possibility. In this chapter, we delve into the transformative power of cultivating a prosperity mindset and explore the strategies and practices that can empower individuals to unlock their full potential and create a legacy of prosperity.

At its core, a prosperity mindset is rooted in the belief that abundance is not limited, but rather abundant resources, opportunities, and possibilities exist for those who embrace a mindset of abundance and abundance consciousness. By adopting a prosperity mindset, individuals shift their focus from scarcity and limitations to abundance and opportunities, thereby opening themselves up to greater possibilities and success.

Throughout this chapter, we will explore the foundational principles of a prosperity mindset and provide practical tools and techniques for cultivating this empowering mindset in your own life. From overcoming limiting beliefs and self-doubt to embracing a mindset of abundance and gratitude, each section of this chapter is designed to help you unlock your innate potential and create a legacy of prosperity that extends far beyond financial wealth.

Moreover, we recognize that cultivating a prosperous mindset is not merely about personal success; it is also about contributing to the greater good and making a positive impact on the world. As you embark on this journey of mindset transformation, we encourage you to consider how your newfound abundance consciousness can be leveraged to uplift others and create a ripple effect of prosperity in your community and beyond.

By embracing a prosperity mindset, you have the power to transcend limitations, overcome challenges, and manifest your deepest desires. As we embark on this transformative journey together, may you be inspired to cultivate a mindset of abundance, resilience, and possibility, and may your legacy be one of prosperity, impact, and lasting significance.

- The Psychology of Wealth

The psychology of wealth delves into the complex interplay between human behavior, attitudes, emotions, and beliefs concerning money, affluence, and financial well-being. Understanding the psychological factors that influence how individuals perceive, manage, and interact with wealth is crucial for fostering financial health, happiness, and long-term prosperity. A comprehensive discussion of the psychology of wealth encompasses various key aspects:

1. Beliefs and Mindsets:

- **Scarcity vs. Abundance Mindset**: Individuals with a scarcity mindset perceive wealth as finite and elusive, leading to feelings of fear, anxiety, and competition. In contrast, those with an abundance mindset view wealth as abundant and attainable, fostering feelings of confidence, gratitude, and collaboration.

- **Money Scripts**: Money scripts are ingrained beliefs and attitudes about money that shape financial behaviors and decisions. These scripts are often formed during childhood and can either empower or limit an individual's relationship with money.

2. Emotions and Money:

- **Emotional Investing**: Emotions such as fear, greed, and overconfidence can influence investment decisions, leading to impulsive behavior, irrational risk-taking, and suboptimal outcomes.

- **Money and Happiness**: While wealth can provide financial security and comfort, research suggests that beyond a certain threshold, additional wealth has diminishing returns on emotional well-being. Factors such as social connections, meaningful work, and personal growth play a more significant role in long-term happiness than material wealth alone.

3. **Behavioral Biases:**

- **Loss Aversion:** People tend to feel the pain of losses more acutely than the pleasure of gains, leading to risk aversion and a reluctance to take necessary financial risks.

- **Confirmation Bias**: Individuals often seek out information that confirms their preexisting beliefs about money and ignore contradictory evidence, leading to a distorted perception of financial reality.

- **Herd Mentality**: People tend to follow the actions of the crowd, even if those actions are irrational or counterproductive, leading to market bubbles and crashes.

4. Wealth and Identity:

- **Self-Worth and Net Worth:** For many individuals, self-worth becomes closely intertwined with net worth, leading to feelings of inadequacy or superiority based on financial status.

- **Social Comparison**: People often compare their wealth and material possessions to others, leading to feelings of envy, insecurity, or status-seeking behavior.

5. Financial Behaviors and Decision-Making:

- **Budgeting and Saving**: Psychological factors such as self-control, impulsivity, and delayed gratification influence one's ability to budget effectively and save for the future.

- **Risk Management**: Tolerance for financial risk varies among individuals and is influenced by factors such as personality traits, past experiences, and cognitive biases.

Understanding the psychology of wealth is essential for promoting financial literacy, resilience, and well-being. By recognizing and addressing the psychological factors that influence financial behaviors and decisions, individuals can cultivate a healthier relationship with money, make more informed choices, and ultimately achieve greater financial security and fulfillment.

- Overcoming Limiting Beliefs and Mindset Blocks

Overcoming limiting beliefs and mindset blocks is a transformative process that involves identifying, challenging, and reframing deeply ingrained thoughts, attitudes, and perceptions that hinder personal growth, success, and fulfillment. These beliefs often stem from past experiences, societal conditioning, and negative self-talk, and can manifest in various aspects of life, including relationships, career, health, and finances. A comprehensive discussion of the process of overcoming limiting beliefs and mindset blocks encompasses several key steps:

1. **Awareness and Identification:**

   - **Recognizing Limiting Beliefs**: The first step in overcoming limiting beliefs is to become aware of their existence. This requires introspection and self-reflection to identify recurring thoughts, narratives, and self-talk patterns that undermine confidence, motivation, and progress.

   - **Understanding Origins**: Explore the origins of limiting beliefs, considering how past experiences, childhood conditioning, and societal influences have shaped your mindset. Recognize that these beliefs may no longer serve you and are based on outdated information or misconceptions.

2. **Challenge and Questioning:**

   - **Critical Inquiry**: Challenge the validity and accuracy of limiting beliefs by questioning their basis in reality. Ask yourself whether there is concrete evidence to support these beliefs or if they are merely assumptions or interpretations.

- **Cognitive Restructuring**: Reframe negative or distorted thoughts into more realistic and empowering perspectives. Replace self-defeating statements with affirmations that affirm your worth, potential, and capacity for growth.

3. **Behavioral Experimentation:**

- **Testing Assumptions**: Experiment with new behaviors, actions, or perspectives that challenge your limiting beliefs. Act as if your desired outcome is already true, and observe how your behavior and experiences change as a result.

- **Incremental Progress**: Start with small, manageable steps and gradually increase the level of challenge as you build confidence and momentum. Celebrate even minor victories and acknowledge your progress along the way.

4. Cultivating Self-Compassion and Resilience:

- **Practice Self-Compassion**: Be gentle and compassionate with yourself as you navigate the process of overcoming limiting beliefs. Recognize that change takes time and effort, and allow yourself to embrace imperfection and setbacks as part of the learning process.

- **Cultivate Resilience**: Develop resilience by adopting a growth mindset and viewing challenges as opportunities for learning and growth. Cultivate resilience through practices such as mindfulness, gratitude, and self-care, which enhance emotional well-being and coping skills.

5. Seeking Support and Accountability:

- **Enlist Support**: Seek guidance and encouragement from friends, family members, mentors, or professionals who can offer perspective, feedback, and support as you work to overcome limiting beliefs.

- **Accountability Partners**: Partner with someone who shares similar goals and aspirations, and hold each other accountable for challenging limiting beliefs and taking positive action towards personal growth and development.

6. Reinforcement and Integration:

- **Consistent Practice**: Integrate new beliefs and perspectives into your daily life through consistent practice and repetition. Engage in activities, rituals, or affirmations that reinforce your newfound empowering beliefs and mindset.

- **Reflect on Progress**: Regularly reflect on your progress and accomplishments, acknowledging the positive changes you've made and the obstacles you've overcome. Celebrate your successes and use them as motivation to continue challenging limiting beliefs and expanding your potential.

In summary, overcoming limiting beliefs and mindset blocks is a dynamic and iterative process that requires self-awareness, courage, and persistence. By challenging negative thought patterns, reframing limiting beliefs, and cultivating self-compassion and resilience, individuals can liberate themselves from the constraints of their past and unleash their full potential for growth, success, and fulfillment.

- Adopting Habits and Practices That Foster Financial Abundance

Adopting habits and practices that foster financial abundance is a transformative journey that involves cultivating a mindset of abundance, implementing practical strategies for wealth-building, and prioritizing long-term financial well-being. A comprehensive discussion of this process encompasses several key steps:

1. **Mindset Shift:**

   - **Cultivate an Abundance Mindset**: Embrace the belief that opportunities for financial success and abundance are abundant and attainable. Shift from a scarcity mindset, which focuses on lack and limitations, to an abundance mindset, which emphasizes possibility, gratitude, and abundance consciousness.

- **Challenge Limiting Beliefs**: Identify and challenge any limiting beliefs or negative self-talk related to money, success, and worthiness. Reframe these beliefs into empowering affirmations that align with your financial goals and aspirations.

2. **Financial Education and Literacy**:

- **Educate Yourself**: Take proactive steps to increase your financial literacy and understanding of key concepts such as budgeting, saving, investing, debt management, and wealth building. Seek out reputable sources of information, such as books, podcasts, courses, and workshops, to enhance your knowledge and skills.

- **Set Clear Financial Goals**: Define specific, measurable financial goals that align with your values, priorities, and aspirations. Whether it's achieving financial independence, saving for retirement, or building a nest egg for your children's education, having clear objectives provides focus and motivation.

3. **Budgeting and Financial Planning:**

   - **Create a Budget**: Develop a realistic budget that accounts for your income, expenses, debts, and savings goals. Track your spending habits and identify areas where you can reduce expenses or reallocate funds toward your financial priorities.

   - **Establish Emergency Savings**: Build an emergency fund to cover unexpected expenses or financial setbacks. Aim to save three to six months' worth of living expenses in a readily accessible account to provide a financial safety net.

4. **Debt Management and Wealth Accumulation**:

   - **Reduce and Eliminate Debt**: Develop a plan to pay down high-interest debt systematically, starting with the highest interest rates first. Explore strategies such as debt consolidation, balance transfers, or negotiating lower interest rates to accelerate debt repayment.

- **Invest Wisely**: Diversify your investment portfolio across various asset classes, such as stocks, bonds, real estate, and alternative investments, to mitigate risk and maximize returns. Consider consulting with a financial advisor to develop an investment strategy tailored to your goals, risk tolerance, and time horizon.

5. **Practicing Discipline and Consistency:**

- **Automate Savings and Investments**: Set up automatic transfers to your savings and investment accounts to ensure consistency and discipline in building wealth over time. Treat saving and investing as non-negotiable expenses, prioritizing them over discretionary spending.

- **Stick to Your Plan:** Stay committed to your financial goals and resist the temptation to deviate from your plan, especially during periods of market volatility or economic uncertainty. Review your progress regularly and make adjustments as needed, but remain focused on the long-term objectives.

6. Gratitude and Generosity:

- **Practice Gratitude**: Cultivate an attitude of gratitude for the abundance and blessings in your life, including financial resources, opportunities, and relationships. Regularly express appreciation for what you have and celebrate your financial successes, no matter how small.

- **Give Back**: Incorporate philanthropy and charitable giving into your financial plan as a way to contribute to causes and organizations that align with your values. Generosity fosters a sense of abundance and fulfillment, enriching both your life and the lives of others.

In summary, adopting habits and practices that foster financial abundance is a holistic process that involves mindset shifts, education, discipline, and gratitude. By cultivating an abundance mindset, increasing financial literacy, setting clear goals, managing debt, investing wisely, practicing discipline, and embracing generosity, individuals can create a solid foundation for long-term financial success and abundance.

CHAPTER 3: ETHICAL STEWARDSHIP AND RESPONSIBLE WEALTH MANAGEMENT

In the pursuit of building a legacy of significance, how we manage and steward our wealth holds profound implications for both our well-being and the broader societal landscape. Ethical stewardship and responsible wealth management are foundational principles that guide individuals in harnessing financial resources for the betterment of themselves, their communities, and future generations. In this chapter, we explore the essential elements of ethical stewardship and responsible wealth management, delving into the principles, practices, and considerations that underpin this transformative approach to financial stewardship.

At its core, ethical stewardship entails the conscientious and principled management of wealth, with a focus on integrity, accountability, and the common good. It transcends mere financial gain, emphasizing the alignment of financial decisions with ethical values, social responsibility, and environmental sustainability. Through responsible wealth management, individuals have the opportunity to wield their financial resources as a force for positive change, fostering economic prosperity, social equity, and environmental stewardship in the process.

Throughout this chapter, we will explore the multifaceted dimensions of ethical stewardship and responsible wealth management, examining the interconnectedness between financial decisions, ethical considerations, and societal impact. From integrating environmental, social, and governance (ESG) criteria into investment strategies to supporting ethical business practices and philanthropic initiatives, each section of this chapter is designed to empower individuals to navigate the complexities of wealth management with integrity and purpose.

Moreover, we recognize that ethical stewardship extends beyond financial considerations to encompass a holistic approach to wealth that encompasses emotional, intellectual, and spiritual dimensions. By cultivating a mindset of abundance, gratitude, and conscious living, individuals can enhance their capacity for ethical decision-making and responsible wealth management, thereby creating a legacy of enduring significance and positive impact.

As we embark on this journey of ethical stewardship and responsible wealth management, let us embrace the opportunity to align our financial resources with our deepest values and aspirations. Through mindful and principled financial stewardship, we have the power to shape a future that reflects our commitment to integrity, compassion, and sustainability. May this chapter inspire and empower you to embrace ethical stewardship as a guiding principle in your journey toward creating a legacy of purpose, prosperity, and social impact?

- The Intersection of Ethics and Wealth

The intersection of ethics and wealth is a complex and multifaceted domain that encompasses the ethical considerations, principles, and dilemmas associated with the acquisition, management, and distribution of wealth. A comprehensive discussion of this intersection involves exploring various key aspects:

1. **Ethical Decision-Making:**

   - **Ethical Standards**: Ethics provide a framework for determining what is morally right or wrong in the context of wealth management. Key ethical principles such as honesty, integrity, fairness, and accountability guide individuals in making responsible financial decisions.

- **Ethical Dilemmas**: Individuals may encounter ethical dilemmas when faced with conflicting interests or values in their financial dealings. Examples include balancing profitability with social responsibility, navigating conflicts of interest, or deciding between short-term gains and long-term sustainability.

2. Wealth Acquisition:

- **Ethical Business Practices:** Wealth acquisition through business endeavors requires adherence to ethical business practices, including transparency, fairness, and respect for stakeholders' interests. Ethical considerations may include labor practices, environmental sustainability, product safety, and corporate governance.

- **Wealth Disparities**: Ethical concerns arise from the growing wealth gap between the affluent and the disadvantaged. Addressing wealth disparities requires a commitment to social justice, equitable distribution of resources, and policies that promote economic mobility and opportunity for all.

3. Wealth Management:

- **Responsible Investment**: Wealth management involves allocating financial resources to various investment vehicles, such as stocks, bonds, real estate, and alternative investments. Responsible investment practices incorporate environmental, social, and governance (ESG) criteria to assess the ethical and sustainability impact of investment decisions.

- **Fiduciary Duty**: Wealth managers, financial advisors, and trustees have a fiduciary duty to act in the best interests of their clients or beneficiaries. This duty requires prioritizing client welfare, avoiding conflicts of interest, and providing transparent and objective advice.

4. Philanthropy and Social Impact:

- **Ethical Philanthropy**: Philanthropic endeavors involve donating wealth to charitable causes and organizations to address social, environmental, or humanitarian issues. Ethical philanthropy requires careful consideration of impact, effectiveness, and accountability to ensure that charitable contributions are used responsibly and ethically.

- **Social Impact Investing**: Social impact investing seeks to generate positive social or environmental outcomes alongside financial returns. Ethical considerations include evaluating the social and environmental impact of investments, promoting sustainable development, and advancing social justice initiatives.

5. Personal Financial Behavior:

- **Financial Integrity**: Personal financial behavior reflects individual values, attitudes, and ethics concerning money management. Ethical financial behavior involves living within one's means, avoiding excessive debt, honoring financial commitments, and prioritizing long-term financial well-being over short-term gratification.

- **Consumer Ethics**: Ethical considerations in consumer behavior include responsible consumption, fair trade practices, and supporting companies that uphold ethical standards in their operations, supply chains, and labor practices.

In summary, the intersection of ethics and wealth encompasses a wide range of ethical considerations and dilemmas inherent in wealth acquisition, management, and distribution. By embracing ethical principles, individuals, businesses, and institutions can contribute to a more just, equitable, and sustainable financial system that promotes the well-being of individuals, communities, and society as a whole.

- Implementing Sustainable Investment Strategies

Implementing sustainable investment strategies involves allocating financial resources to companies, organizations, and projects that promote environmental, social, and governance (ESG) criteria alongside financial returns. A comprehensive discussion of this topic encompasses several key aspects:

1. **Understanding Sustainable Investing**:

 - **ESG Factors**: Sustainable investment strategies consider environmental (E), social (S), and governance (G) factors when evaluating investment opportunities. Environmental factors may include carbon emissions, resource management, and renewable energy. Social factors encompass labor practices, human rights, diversity, and community relations. Governance factors focus on corporate governance, transparency, and ethics.

 - **Integration of Values and Financial Objectives**: Sustainable investing seeks to align investors' values and principles with their financial objectives. Investors may prioritize specific ESG criteria based on their values, ethical considerations, and long-term goals.

2. **Types of Sustainable Investment Strategies:**

 - **Negative Screening**: Negative screening involves excluding companies or industries deemed to have negative social or environmental impacts from the investment portfolio. Examples may include companies involved in fossil fuels, tobacco, weapons, or unethical labor practices.

- **Positive Screening:** Positive screening involves selecting investments based on specific ESG criteria or sustainability themes. Investors may target companies with strong environmental practices, diverse workforces, or innovative solutions to social challenges.

- **ESG Integration**: ESG integration involves incorporating ESG factors into traditional financial analysis to assess investment risks and opportunities more comprehensively. Investors consider how ESG factors may impact a company's financial performance, resilience, and long-term sustainability.

- **Impact Investing**: Impact investing aims to generate measurable social or environmental impact alongside financial returns. Investments may focus on sectors such as renewable energy, affordable housing, healthcare, education, or microfinance, to address pressing societal challenges.

- Shareholder Engagement and Advocacy: Shareholder engagement involves actively engaging with companies on ESG issues through dialogue, proxy voting, and shareholder resolutions. Investors advocate for corporate policies and practices that align with sustainable development goals and promote long-term value creation.

3. Performance and Risk Considerations:

- Financial Performance: Studies have shown that sustainable investment strategies can deliver competitive financial returns over the long term. Companies with strong ESG practices may exhibit better risk management, operational efficiency, innovation, and brand reputation, which can translate into financial outperformance.

- Risk Management: Sustainable investing incorporates non-financial risks, such as regulatory compliance, reputation risk, and climate change, into the investment decision-making process. By addressing these risks proactively, investors can enhance portfolio resilience and reduce downside risk.

4. **Measuring Impact and Reporting**:

- **Impact Metrics**: Investors use various metrics and frameworks to measure the social and environmental impact of their investments. Common frameworks include the United Nations Sustainable Development Goals (SDGs), the Global Reporting Initiative (GRI), and the Sustainability Accounting Standards Board (SASB).

- **Reporting and Transparency**: Transparency and disclosure are essential for communicating the social and environmental impact of sustainable investments to stakeholders. Investors may require companies to report on ESG performance metrics, targets, and progress toward sustainability goals.

5. **Challenges and Opportunities:**

- **Data Availability and Quality**: One challenge in sustainable investing is the availability and quality of ESG data, which can vary across industries and regions. Investors rely on standardized reporting and data providers to assess ESG performance consistently.

- **Regulatory Landscape**: Regulatory frameworks and disclosure requirements related to ESG issues are evolving globally. Investors must stay informed about regulatory developments and integrate regulatory considerations into their investment strategies.

- **Market Growth and Innovation**: The sustainable investing market is experiencing rapid growth and innovation, driven by increasing investor demand, regulatory pressures, and societal trends. Investors have access to a growing range of sustainable investment products, including mutual funds, exchange-traded funds (ETFs), green bonds, and impact funds.

In summary, implementing sustainable investment strategies involves integrating environmental, social, and governance factors into investment decision-making to generate financial returns while promoting sustainable development and positive societal impact. By adopting a holistic approach to investing that considers both financial and non-financial criteria, investors can contribute to a more sustainable and equitable future.

- Navigating the Complexities of Wealth Transfer and Inheritance

Navigating the complexities of wealth transfer and inheritance involves managing the legal, financial, emotional, and interpersonal aspects of passing assets from one generation to the next. A comprehensive discussion of this topic encompasses several key aspects:

1. **Estate Planning and Legal Considerations**:

   - **Wills and Trusts**: Estate planning involves creating legal documents such as wills and trusts to outline how assets will be distributed upon death. Will specify beneficiaries, guardians for minor children, and instructions for asset distribution. Trusts can provide additional flexibility, privacy, and asset protection.

- **Tax Planning**: Estate taxes, inheritance taxes, and gift taxes may apply to wealth transfer depending on jurisdiction and the size of the estate. Tax-efficient estate planning strategies, such as gifting, charitable giving, and trust structures, can help minimize tax liabilities and preserve wealth for heirs.

- **Power of Attorney and Healthcare Directives:** Estate planning also includes appointing individuals to make financial and healthcare decisions on behalf of the individual in case of incapacity. Powers of attorney and healthcare directives designate agents to manage financial affairs and make medical decisions according to the individual's wishes.

2. **Family Dynamics and Communication:**

- **Open Dialogue**: Effective communication among family members is essential for navigating the complexities of wealth transfer and inheritance.

Openly discussing financial matters, estate plans, and expectations can help mitigate misunderstandings, conflicts, and resentment.

- **Addressing Family Dynamics**: Family dynamics, relationships, and intergenerational conflicts may influence estate planning decisions. Considerations such as fairness, equality, and family values should be taken into account when designing wealth transfer strategies.

- **Professional Mediation**: In cases of family disputes or complex family dynamics, professional mediation or counselling may be beneficial in facilitating productive conversations, resolving conflicts, and preserving family harmony.

3. **Financial Planning and Wealth Preservation**:

- **Financial Analysis**: Assessing the financial implications of wealth transfer and inheritance is critical for ensuring the long-term financial security of heirs. Financial planners can evaluate the impact of inheritance on tax obligations, cash flow, investment strategies, and retirement planning.

- **Wealth Preservation Strategies**: Inherited assets may be subject to mismanagement, creditor claims, or unintended consequences if not properly protected. Wealth preservation strategies such as asset protection trusts, insurance, and family governance structures can safeguard assets and preserve wealth for future generations.

4. **Philanthropy and Legacy Planning:**

- **Charitable Giving**: Many individuals incorporate philanthropy into their estate plans as a means of leaving a legacy and supporting causes they care about. Charitable giving vehicles such as donor-advised funds, charitable trusts, and private foundations offer tax benefits and flexibility in charitable giving.

- **Legacy Planning**: Legacy planning goes beyond financial assets to encompass intangible assets such as values, beliefs, and family stories. Individuals may use legacy letters, ethical wills, and family mission statements to articulate their values, pass on wisdom, and foster a sense of connection and purpose among heirs.

5. **Continual Review and Updates**:

- **Life Changes**: Estate plans should be periodically reviewed and updated to reflect changes in life circumstances, family dynamics, tax laws, and financial goals. Major life events such as marriage, divorce, births, deaths, and significant changes in financial status may necessitate revisions to the estate plan.

- **Professional Guidance**: Working with experienced professionals such as estate planning attorneys, financial advisors, and tax specialists is essential for navigating the complexities of wealth transfer and inheritance. These professionals can provide personalized guidance, expertise, and assistance in designing and implementing effective estate planning strategies.

In summary, navigating the complexities of wealth transfer and inheritance requires careful planning, communication, and professional guidance. By addressing legal, financial, emotional, and interpersonal considerations, individuals can ensure a smooth transition of assets and leave a lasting legacy that reflects their values and aspirations.

CHAPTER 4:

INTEGRATING PHILANTHROPY INTO YOUR LEGACY

As individuals contemplate the legacy they wish to leave behind, many find profound meaning and fulfillment in integrating philanthropy into their life's purpose and impact. The concept of philanthropy extends beyond the mere act of charitable giving; it embodies a deep commitment to making a positive difference in the lives of others and contributing to the betterment of society. In this chapter, we explore the transformative power of philanthropy as a cornerstone of legacy building, delving into the principles, strategies, and considerations involved in integrating philanthropy into one's legacy.

At its essence, philanthropy represents a conscious decision to use one's resources, influence, and expertise to address pressing social, environmental, and humanitarian challenges. Whether through financial contributions, volunteerism, advocacy, or social entrepreneurship, philanthropy empowers individuals to create lasting change and leave a meaningful imprint on the world around them.

Throughout this chapter, we will explore the myriad ways in which philanthropy can be integrated into one's legacy, from developing a philanthropic vision and strategy to engaging family members and future generations in the charitable journey. We will examine the diverse forms of philanthropic giving, including direct donations, donor-advised funds, charitable trusts, and private foundations, each offering unique benefits and opportunities for impact.

Moreover, we recognize that philanthropy is not solely about the transfer of financial resources; it is also about the transfer of values, beliefs, and a sense of social responsibility. By integrating philanthropy into their legacy, individuals have the opportunity to instill these core principles in their heirs, cultivating a legacy of compassion, generosity, and civic engagement that transcends generations.

As we embark on this exploration of integrating philanthropy into our legacies, let us embrace the opportunity to make a meaningful difference in the world and leave a lasting legacy of impact and significance. Through strategic philanthropic initiatives, guided by values of compassion, equity, and sustainability, we have the power to create a brighter future for generations to come. May this chapter inspire and empower you to embark on a philanthropic journey that enriches your life, transforms communities, and leaves a legacy of positive change.

- The Power of Giving Back

The power of giving back extends far beyond the act of charitable giving; it encompasses a profound impact on individuals, communities, and society as a whole. A comprehensive discussion of this topic encompasses several key aspects:

1. **Personal Fulfillment and Well-Being:**

- **Sense of Purpose:** Giving back provides individuals with a sense of purpose and meaning, enriching their lives and fostering a deeper connection to their communities and the world.

- **Emotional Satisfaction**: Engaging in philanthropy and acts of kindness promotes feelings of joy, fulfillment, and gratitude, enhancing overall emotional well-being and life satisfaction.

- **Psychological Benefits**: Giving back has been linked to positive psychological outcomes such as increased self-esteem, reduced stress, and improved mental health.

2. **Social Impact and Community Building:**

- **Addressing Social Issues**: Philanthropy addresses pressing social, environmental, and humanitarian challenges, such as poverty, hunger, education inequality, healthcare access, and environmental degradation.

- **Strengthening Communities**: Charitable giving strengthens communities by fostering social cohesion, resilience, and collective action. Philanthropic initiatives bring people together to address shared concerns and build a more equitable and inclusive society.

- **Empowering Marginalized Groups**: Giving back empowers marginalized and underserved populations by providing resources, opportunities, and support to overcome systemic barriers and achieve their full potential.

3. **Promoting Social Change and Innovation:**

- **Catalyzing Social Change**: Philanthropy plays a critical role in driving social change by funding innovative solutions, supporting advocacy efforts, and amplifying the voices of marginalized communities.

- **Encouraging Innovation**: Charitable giving fosters innovation and entrepreneurship by investing in research, technology, and social enterprises that tackle complex societal challenges and create positive change.

- **Leveraging Collective Impact**: Collaborative philanthropic initiatives bring together diverse stakeholders, including nonprofits, businesses, governments, and individuals, to leverage collective resources and expertise for greater impact.

4. **Generational Impact and Legacy Building**:

- **Passing on Values**: Giving back allows individuals to pass on their values, beliefs, and a sense of social responsibility to future generations. Philanthropic families instill a culture of generosity, compassion, and civic engagement that transcends generations.

- **Building a Lasting Legacy**: Philanthropy enables individuals to leave a lasting legacy of positive change and impact. Through strategic giving, donors can create enduring solutions to societal problems and inspire others to continue their philanthropic legacy.

5. Global Citizenship and Responsibility:

- **Promoting Global Solidarity**: Giving back fosters a sense of global citizenship and interconnectedness, encouraging individuals to recognize their responsibility to contribute to the well-being of people and the planet beyond their immediate communities.

- **Addressing Global Challenges**: Philanthropy plays a crucial role in addressing global challenges such as climate change, refugee crises, infectious diseases, and humanitarian emergencies. International philanthropic efforts provide vital support to vulnerable populations and promote global cooperation and solidarity.

In summary, the power of giving back lies in its ability to transform lives, strengthen communities, drive social change, and build a more equitable and sustainable world. By harnessing the collective power of philanthropy, individuals have the opportunity to make a meaningful difference and leave a lasting legacy of impact and compassion.

- Identifying Causes and Organizations That Align with Your Values

The process of identifying causes and organizations that align with your values is a crucial step in effective philanthropy and charitable giving. A comprehensive discussion of this process encompasses several key aspects:

1. Self-Reflection and Clarifying Values:

   - **Start with Self-Reflection**: Take time to reflect on your values, passions, and beliefs. Consider the issues or causes that resonate most deeply with you and reflect on why they are meaningful.

   - **Identify Core Values**: Identify the core values that guide your life and decision-making. These may include principles such as social justice, environmental sustainability, education, healthcare access, human rights, animal welfare, or cultural preservation.

2. Research and Education:

- **Explore Different Causes**: Research a wide range of causes and social issues to gain a deeper understanding of the challenges facing society. Explore topics such as poverty alleviation, environmental conservation, gender equality, racial justice, mental health, and community development.

- **Evaluate Organizational Impact**: Assess the effectiveness, reputation, and impact of nonprofit organizations, charities, and social enterprises working within your areas of interest. Consider factors such as mission alignment, program outcomes, financial transparency, and leadership.

3. Assessing Alignment and Impact:

- **Mission Alignment**: Evaluate the mission, goals, and values of potential causes and organizations to ensure they align with your values and priorities. Look for organizations whose mission resonates with your values and reflects the change you want to see in the world.

- **Programmatic Impact**: Assess the impact and effectiveness of the programs and initiatives implemented by nonprofit organizations. Look for evidence-based practices, measurable outcomes, and success stories that demonstrate the organization's ability to create positive change.

- **Consideration of Scale and Scope**: Consider the scale and scope of the organization's work, as well as its geographic reach and target populations. Determine whether the organization's approach is scalable, sustainable, and capable of addressing systemic issues.

4. **Engagement and Due Diligence:**

- **Connect with Organizations**: Reach out to nonprofit organizations, attend events, or volunteer to learn more about their work and impact firsthand. Engage in dialogue with staff, volunteers, and beneficiaries to gain insights into the organization's values, culture, and effectiveness.

- **Conduct Due Diligence**: Conduct due diligence to assess the credibility, financial health, and governance practices of potential grantees. Review the organization's financial statements, annual reports, governance structure, and IRS Form 990 to ensure transparency and accountability.

5. **Aligning Giving Strategies with Values**:

   - **Strategic Giving**: Develop a strategic giving plan that aligns with your values, priorities, and philanthropic goals. Determine the causes and organizations you wish to support and establish clear criteria for evaluating funding opportunities.

   - **Diversification of Giving**: Consider diversifying your philanthropic portfolio by supporting a mix of causes, organizations, and funding strategies. Explore different types of philanthropic vehicles such as direct donations, donor-advised funds, charitable trusts, and impact investing.

   - **Long-Term Engagement**: Build long-term relationships with the causes and organizations you support by providing sustained funding, volunteerism, and advocacy. Collaborate with grantees to co-create solutions, measure impact, and adapt strategies based on lessons learned.

In summary, the process of identifying causes and organizations that align with your values requires self-reflection, research, due diligence, and strategic engagement. By aligning your giving strategies with your personal values and philanthropic goals, you can maximize the impact of your charitable contributions and create positive change in the world.

- Leveraging Philanthropy as a Catalyst for Social Impact

Leveraging philanthropy as a catalyst for social impact involves strategically deploying financial resources, expertise, and influence to address pressing social, environmental, and humanitarian challenges. A comprehensive discussion of this process encompasses several key aspects:

1. **Strategic Goal Setting:**

   - **Define Social Impact Goals**: Start by clarifying your philanthropic goals and desired outcomes. Identify the social issues or challenges you want to address and establish specific, measurable, achievable, relevant, and time-bound (SMART) goals for creating positive change.

   - **Prioritize Impact Areas**: Prioritize impact areas based on their alignment with your values, expertise, resources, and potential for meaningful change. Focus on areas where you can make a significant difference and leverage your unique strengths and capabilities.

2. **Research and Due Diligence:**

   - **Assess Needs and Opportunities**: Conduct thorough research to understand the root causes and complexities of the social issues you aim to address. Identify gaps, challenges, and opportunities for intervention within the social ecosystem.

   - **Identify Effective Strategies:** Explore evidence-based practices, innovative solutions, and best-in-class interventions that have demonstrated effectiveness in achieving desired social outcomes. Learn from successful models and adapt strategies to fit the local context and community needs.

3. **Partnership and Collaboration**:

 - **Build Strategic Partnerships**: Collaborate with other philanthropists, nonprofit organizations, government agencies, businesses, and community stakeholders to leverage collective resources, expertise, and networks. Form strategic alliances to amplify impact, avoid duplication of efforts, and foster innovation.

 - **Co-Creation and Co-Investment**: Engage stakeholders in the design, implementation, and evaluation of social impact initiatives. Foster a culture of co-creation and co-investment where all partners contribute their unique perspectives, resources, and skills toward shared goals.

4. **Innovation and Experimentation**:

 - **Foster Innovation**: Encourage innovation and experimentation in addressing social challenges by supporting pilot projects, research and development, and social entrepreneurship ventures. Invest in innovative approaches that have the potential to disrupt traditional systems and create transformative change.

- **Embrace Risk and Failure**: Recognize that innovation involves inherent risks and failures. Encourage a culture of learning, adaptation, and resilience, where failures are viewed as opportunities for growth, iteration, and improvement.

5. **Measurement and Evaluation**:

- **Define Metrics for Success**: Establish clear metrics and indicators to measure progress, track outcomes, and assess the effectiveness of social impact initiatives. Use quantitative and qualitative data to evaluate the impact of philanthropic investments and inform decision-making.

- **Continuous Learning and Improvement**: Foster a culture of continuous learning and improvement by regularly reviewing performance data, soliciting feedback from stakeholders, and adapting strategies based on lessons learned. Use evaluation findings to refine approaches, scale successful interventions, and course-correct as needed.

6. **Advocacy and Systems Change**:

   - **Advocate for Policy Change**: Use philanthropic resources and influence to advocate for policy reforms, systemic change, and institutional reforms that address root causes of social problems. Support advocacy efforts that advance social justice, equity, and human rights.

   - **Promote Systems Change**: Invest in initiatives that aim to transform social systems, structures, and norms to create more equitable and inclusive societies. Support efforts to dismantle systemic barriers, promote diversity and inclusion, and build resilience in vulnerable communities.

In summary, leveraging philanthropy as a catalyst for social impact requires strategic goal setting, research and due diligence, partnership and collaboration, innovation and experimentation, measurement and evaluation, advocacy, and systems change. By adopting a strategic and holistic approach to philanthropy, individuals and organizations can maximize their effectiveness in creating positive change and building a more just, equitable, and sustainable world.

CHAPTER 5: NURTURING INTERGENERATIONAL COLLABORATION

In an increasingly interconnected and dynamic world, fostering collaboration across generations is essential for addressing complex societal challenges, driving innovation, and building a more inclusive and sustainable future. Intergenerational collaboration brings together individuals of different ages, backgrounds, and perspectives to exchange ideas, share knowledge, and work together toward common goals. In this chapter, we explore the transformative potential of intergenerational collaboration, examining the benefits, opportunities, and strategies for nurturing meaningful partnerships across generations.

At its core, intergenerational collaboration recognizes the unique contributions and experiences of individuals from different age groups—from youth and young adults to older adults and elders. By harnessing the collective wisdom, energy, and creativity of diverse generations, intergenerational collaboration has the power to generate fresh insights, spark innovation, and drive positive change in communities and society at large.

Throughout this chapter, we will explore the diverse forms and contexts of intergenerational collaboration, from mentorship and knowledge sharing to joint initiatives and community engagement. We will highlight the reciprocal nature of intergenerational relationships, where both younger and older generations have much to teach and learn from each other.

Moreover, we recognize that intergenerational collaboration is not without its challenges, including generational differences in values, communication styles, and technology use. However, by fostering mutual respect, empathy, and open dialogue, these challenges can be overcome, leading to stronger and more resilient intergenerational partnerships.

As we embark on this exploration of nurturing intergenerational collaboration, let us embrace the opportunity to bridge generational divides, celebrate diversity, and harness the collective potential of all age groups. By fostering meaningful connections and collaboration across generations, we can build a more inclusive, equitable, and vibrant society that values the contributions of every individual, regardless of age. May this chapter inspire and empower you to cultivate intergenerational partnerships that foster innovation, promote social cohesion, and create a brighter future for generations to come?

- Fostering Open Dialogue Within Your Family

Fostering open dialogue within your family is essential for building trust, strengthening relationships, and promoting understanding among family members. A comprehensive discussion of this process encompasses several key aspects:

1. Creating a Safe and Supportive Environment:

  - **Establish Trust**: Create an atmosphere of trust and confidentiality where family members feel comfortable expressing their thoughts, feelings, and concerns without fear of judgment or reprisal.

  - **Active Listening**: Practice active listening by giving your full attention to the speaker, maintaining eye contact, and refraining from interrupting or passing judgment. Demonstrate empathy and understanding by validating the speaker's emotions and perspectives.

- **Respectful Communication**: Foster respectful communication by setting ground rules for dialogue, such as speaking respectfully, avoiding personal attacks, and refraining from raising voices or using offensive language.

2. **Initiating and Facilitating Conversations**:

- **Schedule Family Meetings**: Set aside dedicated time for family meetings or discussions to address important topics, make decisions, and resolve conflicts. Regularly scheduled meetings provide a structured forum for open dialogue and collective decision-making.

- **Choose Appropriate Settings**: Select comfortable and neutral settings for family discussions, such as a living room, dining table, or outdoor space, where everyone can gather without distractions or interruptions.

- **Use Icebreakers and Conversation Starters**: Use icebreakers, prompts, or conversation starters to initiate discussions and encourage participation.

Topics may range from shared family memories and traditions to current events, values, and aspirations.

3. Encouraging Transparency and Honesty:

- **Lead by Example**: Model honesty, transparency, and vulnerability in your communication with family members. Share your thoughts, feelings, and experiences openly to encourage others to do the same.

- **Encourage Authenticity**: Create a culture of authenticity and honesty by acknowledging mistakes, expressing vulnerability, and admitting when you don't have all the answers. Embrace imperfection as an opportunity for growth and learning.

4. Navigating Difficult Conversations:

- **Approach with Empathy**: Approach difficult conversations with empathy and compassion, recognizing that different family members may have varying perspectives, experiences, and emotions. Validate their feelings and seek to understand their underlying concerns.

- **Use "I" Statements:** Use "I" statements to express your thoughts and feelings without blaming or accusing others. For example, say "I feel hurt when..." instead of "You always make me feel..."

- **Focus on Solutions**: Shift the focus of difficult conversations from blame and criticism to collaborative problem-solving and finding mutually acceptable solutions. Brainstorm ideas together and explore compromises that address the needs and concerns of all parties involved.

5. **Resolving Conflicts Constructively**:

- **Practice Active Listening:** Listen attentively to each party's perspective, restate their concerns to ensure understanding, and seek common ground for resolution.

- **Seek Mediation or Facilitation**: In cases of unresolved conflicts or impasses, consider involving a neutral third party, such as a mediator, counselor, or family therapist, to facilitate communication, manage emotions, and guide the negotiation process.

- Focus on Reconciliation and Healing: Prioritize reconciliation and healing by acknowledging the impact of the conflict on family relationships, expressing forgiveness, and committing to rebuilding trust and understanding.

6. Celebrating Diversity and Differences:

- Embrace Diversity: Celebrate the diversity of perspectives, experiences, and identities within your family. Recognize that differences enrich relationships and provide opportunities for learning, growth, and mutual respect.

- Foster Inclusion: Create an inclusive environment where every family member feels valued, accepted, and appreciated for who they are. Encourage open-mindedness, empathy, and curiosity about others' backgrounds and perspectives.

In summary, fostering open dialogue within your family requires creating a safe and supportive environment, initiating and facilitating conversations, encouraging transparency and honesty, navigating difficult conversations with empathy and respect, resolving conflicts constructively, and celebrating diversity and differences. By cultivating open communication and mutual understanding, families can build stronger, more resilient relationships and navigate challenges with greater cohesion and unity.

- Passing Down Values, Wisdom, and Lessons Learned

Passing down values, wisdom, and lessons learned is a deeply meaningful and essential aspect of family life. A comprehensive discussion of this process encompasses several key aspects:

1. **Identifying Core Values and Beliefs:**

   - **Self-Reflection**: Begin by reflecting on your core values, beliefs, and life lessons. Consider the principles and ideals that have guided you throughout your life and shaped your identity.

- **Family Values Assessment**: Engage family members in discussions about shared values, beliefs, and cultural traditions. Explore the origins and significance of family values and identify those that are most important to preserve and pass down to future generations.

2. **Creating Opportunities for Transmission**:

- **Storytelling and Oral Tradition**: Share family stories, anecdotes, and personal experiences with younger generations to impart wisdom and values in a meaningful and engaging way. Use storytelling as a vehicle for transmitting cultural heritage, life lessons, and moral teachings.

- **Rituals and Traditions**: Establish family rituals, traditions, and ceremonies that reinforce values, celebrate milestones, and strengthen intergenerational bonds. Create meaningful rituals around holidays, birthdays, family gatherings, and special occasions that foster a sense of belonging and continuity.

- **Formal and Informal Education**: Provide formal and informal opportunities for learning and dialogue about values, ethics, and life skills. Incorporate discussions about values and character development into everyday activities, such as mealtime conversations, family outings, and bedtime routines.

3. **Leading by Example**:

- **Role Modeling:** Serve as a role model for younger generations by living according to your values and demonstrating integrity, compassion, and resilience in your actions and decisions. Model positive behaviors, attitudes, and habits that reflect the values you wish to instill in others.

- **Teachable Moments**: Seize teachable moments in everyday life to reinforce values and impart wisdom. Use real-life situations, challenges, and opportunities as opportunities for learning and growth, offering guidance, support, and encouragement along the way.

4. Encouraging Critical Thinking and Reflection:

- **Engage in Dialogue**: Encourage open dialogue and critical thinking among family members about values, ethics, and moral dilemmas. Create a safe and supportive environment where individuals can express their opinions, ask questions, and explore different perspectives.

- **Foster Self-Reflection**: Encourage self-reflection and introspection among family members to deepen their understanding of themselves, their values, and their place in the world. Encourage journaling, mindfulness practices, and self-assessment exercises that promote self-awareness and personal growth.

5. Adapting to Changing Times:

- **Evolving Values**: Recognize that values and beliefs may evolve in response to changing social, cultural, and environmental contexts. Be open to revisiting and reevaluating family values in light of new experiences, insights, and challenges.

- **Embrace Diversity**: Embrace diversity and inclusivity by respecting and valuing differences in values, beliefs, and perspectives among family members. Encourage dialogue and mutual understanding across generational, cultural, and ideological divides.

6. **Promoting Intergenerational Learning and Exchange**:

- **Bridge Generational Divides**: Facilitate intergenerational learning and exchange by creating opportunities for older and younger family members to connect, share experiences, and learn from each other. Foster mutual respect, empathy, and understanding across generations.

- **Mentorship and Guidance**: Encourage mentoring relationships between older and younger family members, where wisdom, skills, and knowledge are passed down from one generation to the next. Create mentorship programs or pairings that facilitate learning, growth, and personal development.

In summary, the process of passing down values, wisdom, and lessons learned involves identifying core values and beliefs, creating opportunities for transmission, leading by example, encouraging critical thinking and reflection, adapting to changing times, and promoting intergenerational learning and exchange. By actively engaging in this process, families can preserve their cultural heritage, strengthen their bonds, and empower future generations to lead purposeful and values-driven lives.

- Collaborating Across Generations to Sustain and Enhance Your Legacy

Collaborating across generations to sustain and enhance your legacy is a dynamic and enriching process that involves leveraging the collective wisdom, energy, and resources of family members from different age groups. A comprehensive discussion of this process encompasses several key aspects:

1. **Shared Vision and Purpose**:

   - **Define Shared Goals**: Engage family members in discussions to articulate a shared vision and purpose for sustaining and enhancing your legacy. Identify common values, aspirations, and long-term goals that reflect the collective identity and aspirations of the family.

   - **Foster Alignment**: Ensure alignment between individual aspirations and the collective vision by facilitating open dialogue, active listening, and consensus-building among family members. Encourage participation from all generations to promote inclusivity and ownership of the shared legacy.

2. **Interdisciplinary Collaboration:**

   - **Harness Diverse Perspectives**: Recognize the value of diverse perspectives, skills, and experiences across generations. Encourage collaboration between family members with different backgrounds, expertise, and interests to enrich decision-making and problem-solving.

- **Foster Cross-Generational Mentorship**: Facilitate mentorship and knowledge transfer between older and younger family members to leverage the wisdom of experience and the fresh insights of youth. Create opportunities for skill-sharing, learning exchanges, and mutual support across generations.

3. **Communication and Transparency**:

- **Promote Open Dialogue**: Cultivate a culture of open communication, transparency, and trust within the family. Create channels for regular dialogue, such as family meetings, newsletters, and online forums, to keep all generations informed and engaged in decision-making processes.

- **Share Information and Updates**: Keep family members informed about the family's history, values, assets, and plans for the future. Provide education opportunities and awareness-building around financial literacy, estate planning, philanthropy, and other topics relevant to sustaining the family legacy.

4. **Collaborative Decision-Making**:

   - **Embrace Consensus-Building**: Embrace a collaborative approach to decision-making that involves seeking input, gathering feedback, and reaching consensus among family members. Encourage democratic processes that empower all generations to contribute to major decisions that impact the family legacy.

   - **Respectful Conflict Resolution**: Recognize that conflicts and disagreements are natural and inevitable in family dynamics. Foster a culture of respectful conflict resolution by providing space for differing viewpoints, active listening, and constructive dialogue to find mutually acceptable solutions.

5. **Capacity Building and Succession Planning**:

   - **Invest in Education and Development**: Invest in the education, training, and development of future leaders within the family. Provide opportunities for skill-building, leadership development, and mentorship programs that prepare younger generations to assume leadership roles and steward the family legacy.

- **Formalize Succession Plans**: Develop formal succession plans and governance structures to ensure continuity and stability in the management and governance of family assets and enterprises. Clearly define roles, responsibilities, and decision-making processes to facilitate smooth transitions across generations.

6. **Celebrating Achievements and Milestones:**

- **Recognize Contributions**: Acknowledge and celebrate the contributions and achievements of family members across generations. Create rituals, ceremonies, and traditions that honor milestones, such as graduations, weddings, births, and career milestones, as well as family anniversaries and reunions.

- **Preserve Family Stories**: Preserve and pass down family stories, traditions, and artefacts that capture the essence of the family legacy and heritage. Documenting and sharing these stories fosters a sense of continuity, connection, and identity across generations.

In summary, collaborating across generations to sustain and enhance your legacy involves defining shared goals and purpose, harnessing diverse perspectives through interdisciplinary collaboration, promoting open communication and transparency, embracing collaborative decision-making, investing in education and development, formalizing succession plans, and celebrating achievements and milestones. By engaging in this collaborative process, families can preserve their legacy, strengthen intergenerational bonds, and empower future generations to carry forward their shared values and aspirations.

CONCLUSION

In the concluding pages of "Legacy Builders: Creating Wealth for Future Generations," we find ourselves at the intersection of reflection and action, where the journey of wealth creation meets the timeless pursuit of leaving a lasting legacy. Throughout this book, we have explored the multifaceted dimensions of legacy building, delving into the intricacies of financial stewardship, intergenerational collaboration, and the profound impact of values-driven decision-making.

As we bring our exploration to a close, it is essential to recognize that the true measure of wealth extends far beyond material possessions and financial assets. Indeed, the legacy we leave behind is shaped not only by the wealth we accumulate but also by the values we uphold, the relationships we nurture, and the impact we make on the world around us.

In the pursuit of building a legacy that transcends generations, we have uncovered valuable insights and practical strategies for creating wealth with purpose and intentionality. We have learned that true wealth lies in aligning our financial goals with our deepest values, fostering open dialogue and collaboration within our families, and embracing a mindset of abundance and generosity.

As we look to the future, let us carry forward the lessons learned from this journey and commit ourselves to being stewards of prosperity, both for ourselves and for future generations. Let us continue to invest in relationships, cultivate wisdom, and empower others to realize their full potential.

In closing, "Legacy Builders" serves as a roadmap for those who aspire to create a legacy of impact, integrity, and enduring significance. May this book inspire and empower you to embark on your journey of legacy building, knowing that the legacy you create today has the power to shape the world for generations to come.